5623 9295

A Penguin Named Patience

A Hurricane Katrina Rescue Story

Suzanne Lewis • Illustrated by Lisa Anchin

To Jennie Newton who took me to see the penguins,
Tom Dyer who explained their ordeal,
and librarian Kim Wood who said that would make a terrific picture book.
—Suzanne

For Mom, Dad, and Dina
—Lisa

ILLUSTRATOR ACKNOWLEDGMENTS
With special thanks to Ezra for his unending encouragement;
to Jo for all of her support; and to all of the Mentees for being my tribe;
but especially to David and Gabrielle Diaz, Maple Lam, and Brooke Boynton-Hughes
for accompanying me on the first early reference-gathering trip to the aquarium.

Sleeping Bear Press gratefully acknowledges and thanks Tom Dyer and Katie Smith at
Audubon Aquarium of the Americas in New Orleans for their review of and help with the story.

FedEx is a trademark of Federal Express Corporation.
Airbus is a registered trademark of Airbus S.A.S.

Sleeping Bear Press™

315 E. Eisenhower Pkwy., Suite 200
Ann Arbor, MI 48108
www.sleepingbearpress.com

Printed and bound in the United States.
10 9 8 7 6 5 4 3 2 1
Library of Congress Cataloging-in-Publication Data

Lewis, Suzanne, 1954- author.
A penguin named Patience : a Hurricane Katrina rescue story
written by Suzanne Lewis ; illustrated by Lisa Anchin.
pages cm
Summary: "Patience is a South African penguin living at New Orleans's
Audubon Aquarium of the Americas. When the Aquarium is severely damaged
during Hurricane Katrina, many animals are put in peril, including
Patience and the other penguins. They must leave their home, and their
penguin keeper, until it is restored"-- Provided by publisher.
ISBN 978-1-58536-840-2
1. African penguin--Louisiana--New Orleans--Juvenile literature. 2.
Hurricane Katrina, 2005--Juvenile literature. 3. Animal rescue--Juvenile
literature. 4. Penguins--Juvenile literature. 5. New Orleans
(La.)--Juvenile literature. I. Anchin, Lisa, illustrator. II. Title.
QL696.S473L49 2015
598.4709763'35--dc23
2014016870

Patience knew something was terribly wrong.

It was dark and steamy hot inside her home at Audubon Aquarium in New Orleans. Being an African penguin meant she was used to a warm climate, but not this warm!

Outside, the weather was dreadful. Hurricane Katrina had battered New Orleans. The aquarium staff was evacuated because of flooding. The electricity was off everywhere. Inside the penguin exhibit, the air grew dangerously hotter.

Where was Tom, the penguin keeper, with his pail of sardines? He was always there to scratch her neck and feed her twice a day.

Patience tried to be patient.

Being the oldest, Patience had to keep all her penguins in line.

Fanny was grumpy. Ernie was snippy. Kohl was red hot. Bunny was jumpy. Amquel was stinky. Voodoo was under a spell. Rocky was punchy. Satchmo was bored. Dyer was dire. Zelda was Zelda. Dennis was a menace.

And Patience tried to be patient.

Just as she headed into her little cave, a flashlight blinked around the corner. "One . . . two . . . three . . . four . . . five . . . six . . ." Then, ". . . sixteen . . . seventeen . . . eighteen . . ."

It was Tom!

". . . and Patience makes nineteen. Oh, thank goodness you are all okay! We've got to get you out of here. I'm just not sure how."

Patience didn't let Tom out of her sight.
He offered her some sardines, but she felt
too nervous. He did what he could to make
things cooler.

Patience tried to be patient.

Patience was scared. Her home was such a mess. But Tom promised her everything would be okay.

He helped the penguins get ready. "You all are going on a long trip! You'll meet new penguin friends. They are waiting for you at the Monterey Bay Aquarium. Just as soon as this place gets fixed, we'll figure out a way to bring you home."

In her cage, Patience was confused and worried. She was relieved to see Tom getting on the plane, too. He tried to comfort all the nervous penguins.

When they arrived at their new aquarium, Patience was happy to have Tom with them. The New Orleans penguins were quarantined for a short time to make sure they weren't contagious. Then all the penguins enjoyed swimming together and meeting one another.

But after a while, Tom needed to leave.
He promised Patience he'd be waiting
for her at the New Orleans aquarium
just as soon as it was restored.

Patience tried to be patient.

Even with Tom gone,
    Patience was happy.

She liked swimming in a cool
aquarium again. She liked making
new penguin friends. And she enjoyed
all the people who came to see the visiting
penguins from New Orleans.

It took nine months for their aquarium home in
New Orleans to be fixed. When it was ready,
a FedEx Airbus flew Patience and her friends back home.

True to his word, Tom was there
to greet her. He climbed aboard and
picked her up. "Hi, sweetheart," he cooed.

FedEx rolled out the purple carpet and Patience waddled down it to a band playing "When the Saints Go Marching In."

Finally, she was home again.

And all it took was a little patience.

Author's Note

Hurricane Katrina inflicted tragedy of monumental proportions on the people of New Orleans and the southeast in August 2005. Katrina's storm surge caused several breaches in levees around New Orleans. Most of the city was subsequently flooded, as the breached drainage and navigation canals allowed water to flow from the lake into low areas of the city. Tragically, many lives were lost in the hurricane and subsequent floods, making it the deadliest U.S. hurricane since the 1928 Okeechobee hurricane.

Though Audubon Aquarium of the Americas survived the initial hurricane and was on high ground above the flooding of most of the city, electrical outages continued and the backup power generators were unable to fully operate the sophisticated life support systems needed.

Sadly, many aquatic animals perished but thanks to a dedicated staff, fortunately the aquarium's sea otters, macaws and raptors, leafy and weedy sea dragons, some fishes, green sea turtles, and 19 penguins survived.

Monterey Aquarium in California generously assisted Audubon Aquarium by offering to house the displaced penguin colony. Audubon's Senior Aviculturist accompanied the penguins on a cargo plane to their temporary home in California to join the resident penguins on exhibit in Monterey.

Monterey Aquarium's 18 own penguins originally came from New Orleans so this was a family reunion of sorts for the rescued Audubon penguins.

They quickly adapted to their temporary home while Audubon Aquarium was refurbished. Nine months later, FedEx donated $100,000 and a chartered flight to fly the penguins home.

Audubon Aquarium of the Americas was saddened by the loss of Patience the Penguin in 2006; she had lived to be 25. The mean life expectancy of male African penguins is 17.3 years and 15.1 years for female African penguins. Patience had the best care and all the love in the world.